T0279581

IMAGES
of America

THE LINCOLN
FUNERAL TRAIN

The engineer (front, holding oil can) poses with officials of the Pennsylvania Railroad and dignitaries riding the Lincoln funeral train at the West Philadelphia station. Locomotive No. 331 is festooned with flags and mourning bunting. (Library of Congress.)

ON THE COVER: One of the most noted photographs taken during the run of the funeral train is of the elaborately decorated *Nashville* parked outside Cleveland's Union Station. Railroad crewmen and dignitaries associated with the Lincoln funeral train pose proudly around the locomotive. (Library of Congress.)

IMAGES
of America

THE LINCOLN
FUNERAL TRAIN

Michael Leavy

ARCADIA
PUBLISHING

Copyright © 2023 by Michael Leavy
ISBN 978-1-4671-0952-9

Published by Arcadia Publishing
Charleston, South Carolina

Printed in the United States of America

Library of Congress Control Number: 2022948015

For all general information, please contact Arcadia Publishing:
Telephone 843-853-2070
Fax 843-853-0044
E-mail sales@arcadiapublishing.com
For customer service and orders:
Toll-Free 1-888-313-2665

Visit us on the Internet at www.arcadiapublishing.com

For my twin brother, Glenn. We were born on Lincoln's birthday, a minor thing that nonetheless heightened our appreciation of America's remarkable story.

CONTENTS

ACKNOWLEDGMENTS

I would like to thank the Library of Congress for making its collection of Civil War images, documents, and maps available to the public. It is a fascinating experience moving back and forth in time through the various collections so wonderfully preserved. I would also like to thank Caroline (Anderson) Vickerson at Arcadia Publishing for guiding me through the production of this book.

INTRODUCTION

The Civil War stressed America morally, financially, politically, and spiritually as nothing has before or since. What was to be a quick war—an adventure young men ran to enlist in—quickly ranged out of control into a catastrophic bloodbath lasting from 1861 to 1865. It yielded nearly 800,000 military and civilian casualties, reduced numerous Southern cities and towns to rubble, created thousands of destitute orphans, and entrenched painful resentments that would last for generations. It was a war unlike the world had ever seen. Both sides started by attempting to destroy their rival's seat of power, the capital in Washington, DC, and the Confederate capital in Richmond, Virginia. It was one of the first wars in which trains were used, and they escalated, prolonged, and led to much of its carnage. Unlike old Napoleonic warfare where armies battled until one side was annihilated, now trains could move troops and supplies in and out of battles quickly. It was a war that would have destroyed a lesser nation. The fact that the nation survived, reunited, and proved its resilience should be forever inspiring.

The surrender of Confederate general Robert E. Lee's army to Gen. Ulysses S. Grant at Appomattox, Virginia, on April 9, 1865, signaled the end of the war, although there were still active armies in various theaters. It was the end as far as Lincoln was concerned. He went to Richmond and sat at the desk of his vanquished rival, acting president Jefferson Davis.

Lincoln's inner circle noted that they had not seen him as happy and relaxed as they did the morning of April 14, 1865, as he took a coach ride with his beloved wife, Mary. The weight of the war seemingly slipped from his shoulders by the hour as the two spoke of traveling. Lincoln expressed a desire see the Holy Land. There was, however, unseen in the background, the machinery of a plot to kill the president, vice president, secretary of war, and General Grant. The conspirators' attempt to topple the federal government and inspire the defeated South to rekindle its war of secession went somewhat awry, but not before savagely wounding Secretary of State William H. Seward and killing President Lincoln.

This final tragedy came only five days after the end of the war, when Americans were beginning to contemplate that peace was truly upon them. It was also Good Friday and preparations for Easter had been well underway. There was already a heightened spiritual mood that night when the Lincolns laughingly rushed up the stairs to the State Box at Ford's Theater to watch the play *Our American Cousin*. Being late, the play was paused to allow for a spirited welcome from the audience. Noticeably lighthearted, the Lincolns took their seats beside their guests, Maj. Henry Rathbone and his fiancé, Clara Harris. Abraham and Mary leaned over and whispered simple endearments to one another. With the war no longer between them, they were finding their way back to each other.

It was during a line in the play that elicited the loudest laugh that John Wilkes Booth pushed into the box and fired a bullet into Lincoln's head. The half-ounce lead ball traveled diagonally through the president's brain and lodged over his right eye. The impact caused him to squeeze Mary's hand. The assassin was a man the Lincolns admired as an actor and had tried repeatedly to form a friendship with.

The president was taken from the theater to Petersen House across the street, where he died at 7:22 the next morning. He was likely brain dead by midnight, but the puncturing of a clot inside the wound with a probe extended his organ functions.

Telegraph lines quickly carried the news that the president had been killed. This new disaster blended with the already intense spirituality of Easter and the end of the war. A nearly unbearable agony set in. Lincoln was the most hated man in America, especially by women who lost their sons, brothers, husbands, and fathers in what they felt was his needlessly protracted and bungled war. These feelings abated, however, and vengeful thoughts directed at the conquered South would be dealt with later. For now, the Great Emancipator, murdered in his hour of triumph, was going to get a royal send-off worthy of an emperor.

Devastated and confused, Mary Lincoln let herself be badgered into allowing a national series of events spread out over three weeks wherein Americans could mourn and memorialize her husband. There would be funeral processions, music, and public viewing of the corpse. The centerpiece of the pageant would be a spectacular train to carry her husband's and son's remains back to Springfield, Illinois. She could not bring herself to travel with the train, dubbed the Lincoln Special. Instead, she remained in her bedroom at the White House for five weeks ranting, sobbing, and worrying about the odors her husband's decomposing body might exhale. The United States Military Railroad division that oversaw train operations during the war quickly organized the railroads that would participate in the 1,654-mile journey. The route through seven states was, except for a few changes, the reverse of Lincoln's inaugural train ride that brought him to the capital in 1861.

The railroads provided their finest engines and passenger cars. The recently completed presidential coach christened the *United States* was modified to hold Lincoln's casket. All locomotives and cars were adorned with black mourning fabric and patriotic bunting. It was a great honor for all engine crews to be a part of this, and they wore their finest clothes. Citizens traveled many miles to glimpse the train, often camping near the tracks with enormous bonfires illuminating the countryside. A pilot train consisting of a locomotive and single car preceded the funeral train by 10 minutes to make sure all crossings were clear. There had been threats to derail the train. Propelled by train and telegraph, the Lincoln Special steamed through 180 cities and towns and was viewed by nearly three million mourners.

A competition to outdo the previous city in grandeur developed as news accounts were telegraphed ahead. The South found dragging the corpse halfway across the country morbid. Other states, jealously wanting to be somehow involved, held mock funerals.

Ultimately, it was the train that would transcend all the tears, eulogies, and uncertainty, as it became a moving symbol of the nation's sturdiness. At every station it stopped, the tolling of bells gave a transcendental if not providential air to the event. America's love affair with railroads had been immediate starting in the 1830s. They navigated the nation through the Industrial Revolution. In the case of the Lincoln funeral train, its slow steady passing assured millions that the future was bright. Americans would shake off much of Europe's influence on their culture and develop their own approaches to architecture, music, education, art, science, and literature. Lincoln was a railroad lawyer and train man at heart. He would possibly have been bemused at all the fuss. In the manner of trains that come and go, he would have wanted the nation to just move on and put all this behind it.

One

THAT HORRIBLE DAWN

Railroads unexpectedly drove the Civil War, enlarging and lengthening it because they transported soldiers and supplies 10 times faster than beasts of burdens. Afterwards, the railroads, which had inflated the war then brought about its end, were called on for one final service. They were to take the remains of slain Pres. Abraham Lincoln and his son Willie home to their final rests in Springfield, Illinois. (Library of Congress.)

The Lincolns wanted more than just for Abraham to be a successful Springfield lawyer. They wanted to be the toast of Chicago, Boston, and New York. Mary Todd, with the advantage of finishing schools, spruced him up for his political journey. They made it from a second-floor law office to the White House. Ultimately, it proved to be a terrible case of be careful what you wish for. (Both, author's collection.)

This warm and fatherly image of Lincoln with his son Tad is the only one of approximately 130 images of the president that shows the merest indication of a smile. Only stoic gazes were recommended for photographs in that era. (Library of Congress.)

This 1865 oil painting, *The Lincoln Family* by Francis Bicknell Carpenter, was widely reproduced. From left to right are Mary Lincoln, Willie (whom Carpenter added since Willie had died in 1862 of typhoid), Robert (standing behind table), and Tad beside his father. Little is known of their fourth son Edward, who died a month before his fourth birthday in 1850. Only Robert survived to adulthood. (Library of Congress.)

Only seven years separate these portraits of President Lincoln. The one on the right was taken shortly before his death and shows how the stress of war ravaged him physically. (Courtesy Richard Panke.)

Thomas Lincoln, Abraham's father, was an illiterate carpenter and farmer who struggled to support his family. When Abraham's mother died, Thomas married Sarah (Bush) Johnson, a widow with three children. Thomas eventually moved his enlarged family to Illinois, where Abraham spent much of his youth. (Library of Congress.)

Emilie Helm, half-sister to Mary Todd, wrote of a painful meeting with Mary and the president in which they were so grieved by loss of three brothers and Emilie's husband in service to the Confederacy as well as Willie's death in 1862 from typhoid, that they could only speak in choked voices. In a later encounter, Emilie wrote, "Mr. Lincoln put his arms around me, and we both wept." (Author's collection.)

Abraham Lincoln's stepmother, Sarah (Bush) Johnson, married his father in 1819. The joined families moved to the Lincoln family farm in Illinois, where the nine of them lived in a one-room cabin. Upon learning of Abraham's murder, she said "I knowed they'd kill him. I ben awaiting fur it." (Author's collection.)

Lincoln's assassin, John Wilkes Booth, was from a prominent Maryland family of actors. The Lincolns admired his talent and repeatedly invited him to the White House, but he never responded. A brash white supremacist and Confederate activist, he was tracked down and killed on April 26, 1865. (Library of Congress.)

Ford's Theater, built in 1833 as a meetinghouse for the First Baptist Church of Washington, DC, became a theater in 1863. It was here that Lincoln was shot on April 14, 1865. Afterwards, it was taken over by the government and used as a warehouse. A section of the three floors collapsed in 1892, killing 22 clerks and injuring 68 others. It was restored and reopened as a theater in 1968. (Library of Congress.)

The State Box, or President's Box as it was sometimes referred to, is shown here two days after the shooting. The photograph is attributed to a noted photographer of the day, Mathew Brady. A portrait of George Washington was placed between the smaller draped flags. (Library of Congress.)

In an accurate depiction of the shooting, Lincoln's guests are seated on the right. Booth had expressed his hatred of Lincoln in a letter to his sister: "That man's appearance, his pedigree, his frivolity, his low coarse jokes and anecdotes, his vulgar smiles, and his policies are a disgrace to the office he holds. He was made the tool of the North to crush out slavery." (Author's collection.)

Maj. Henry Rathbone and fiancée Clara Harris were guests in the box. Rathbone struggled with Booth and received a dagger cut to his left arm. Afterwards, as US consul in Germany, Rathbone's mental health deteriorated, partially from guilt over the assassination. In 1883, he killed his wife, Clara. Servants got his children away before he could kill them. He died in an asylum in 1911. (Library of Congress.)

Actress Laura Keene (born Mary Francis Moss) was a British actress and theater manager. She was performing in the play *Our American Cousin* when Lincoln was shot. She made her way to the State Box and cradled the president's head in her lap. She would later display her blood-stained dress for profit. (Library of Congress.)

Dr. Charles Leale was the first person with any medical experience to reach Lincoln after he was shot. A 23-year-old Union army doctor, Leale had graduated just six weeks earlier from Bellevue Hospital Medical College. He resuscitated the president even though he knew the wound was mortal. (Library of Congress.)

It was determined that the president would not be allowed to die in a theater. A trip back to the White House would have been agonizing. Instead, Doctors Leale and Charles Sabin Taft had him carried across the street to the Petersen House, a boardinghouse, where he was placed on a bed in a back bedroom. (Library of Congress.)

As the deathwatch continued, Mary Lincoln's hysterical sobbing intensified, causing Secretary of War Edwin M. Stanton to shout, "Take that woman out of here and do not let her back in here again!" Abraham Lincoln was most likely brain dead by midnight. Piercing a clot behind the bullet with a probe kept him alive. It would have been more merciful to just let him die. (Author's collection.)

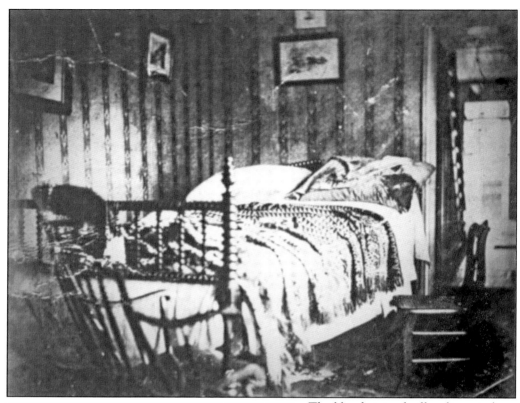

The blood-stained pillow lies grimly on the bed where Lincoln died. The bullet caused brain hemorrhaging, and swelling put pressure on the brain stem, forcing the brain toward the spine. Lincoln may have been saved today, but would have been blind in his right eye and suffered trouble speaking and unsteadiness. He could not have remained president. (Author's collection.)

John Milton Hay was Lincoln's private secretary. Living in the White House, Hay was a constant friend and confidant. He was at Lincoln's bedside when he was pronounced dead that horrible dawn. He became a noted statesman, serving in Republican administrations, including McKinley's—another president to be assassinated. Hay was also a skilled writer. He was a passenger on both the Lincoln Special and the inaugural train. (Author's collection.)

This was the White House in the 1860s when the Lincolns occupied it. The capital was formally called Washington City back then, but is rarely chronicled as such. It was an unbearably hot place, with a thick, swampish atmosphere. Most inhabitants abandoned it in the summer for cooler places, returning when Congress came back into session. (Author's collection.)

This photograph is generally believed to be of Charles Forbes, footman, assistant, and messenger to the Lincolns. Eyewitnesses place him guarding the door leading up to the State Box. Accounts claim Forbes recognized John Wilkes Booth and let him in. Mary Lincoln blamed him for her husband's death and never forgave him. (Author's collection.)

Mary Todd was called a traitor by Southern newspapers after marrying Abraham Lincoln. Northern newspapers viciously attacked her as nasty and emotionally unstable. Mindful of her children, the press was kinder after the assassination, referring to her "frail sensitivities," but Washington society immediately rejected her after the funeral and wanted her out of the White House. (Library of Congress.)

The mobile office car built so Lincoln could meet with governors and state officials after the war is pictured outside the car shops at Alexandria, Virginia. Called the *United States*, it was perhaps the most richly appointed railcar in America, with posh furniture and heating system. It would be comparable to today's Air Force One. It became, however, the hearse car for Lincoln's journey to Springfield. (Library of Congress.)

The conspirators intended to kill Vice Pres. Andrew Johnson, pictured here, but his assigned assassin, George Atzerodt, got drunk and lost his courage. Mary Lincoln believed Johnson was in on the plot. She wrote that her "own intense misery, has been augmented by the same thought—that, that miserable inebriate Johnson, had cognizance of [her] husband's death." (Library of Congress.)

Though not a supporter of Lincoln, Edwin Stanton performed brilliantly as his secretary of war, organizing seemingly impossible logistical systems to move great armies to the fronts. At Mary Lincoln's behest, he became the primary manager of the national funeral she finally agreed to. With Lincoln gone, Democrat newspapers directed their political fire at Stanton, even blaming him for the deterioration of the corpse over the long journey. (Library of Congress.)

Edwin Booth, pictured with daughter Edwina, was John Wilkes Booth's brother and certainly the better of the two. Edwin had saved Lincoln's son Robert's life when both stood on a crowded railroad platform. Robert had been forced to steady himself against a boxcar, which suddenly moved. Edwin grabbed his collar and pulled him back from falling to certain death. (Library of Congress.)

The terrible night of Lincoln's assassination continued when Lewis Powell burst into Secretary Seward's bedroom. Seward, pictured here, had been recovering from a serious fall when Powell stabbed the secretary in front of his daughter, who was attending to him. The disfigurement from the attack is evident in the image at right. It was the last photograph Seward ever allowed. (Both, author's collection.)

Funeral services at the White House were held in the East Room on August 19. The crowd of 600 spilled over into the Green Room. General Grant, in full uniform, sat alone at the head of the catafalque, his face awash in tears. Senate chaplain Phineas Densmore Gurley, depicted here, presided. Inconsolable, Mary did not attend. Simultaneous memorial services were held across the country. (Library of Congress.)

Washington, DC, looks rather serene in this Civil War–era photograph, but it was perhaps the most fortified city in the world, encircled with redoubts, forts, and massive guns aimed up the Potomac River. Approximately 100 miles south stood the bravely defended but nonetheless fallen Confederate capital of Richmond, the city chosen for its Tredegar Iron Works. (Library of Congress.)

The Reverend Doctor Gurley, who served as chaplain of the US Senate, was a close friend of the president and his spiritual advisor as well. He counseled Lincoln when, nearly broken by grief over the loss of his son Willie, he began to question his faith. Gurley would travel with the funeral train. (Author's collection.)

The Treasury Building still has the look of newness about it in this stereo view. A group of prominent Washington citizens is seated beneath the portico observing the city's impressive funeral. Funeral rites where individuals and communities externalize their grief have occurred since the dawn of civilization. (Library of Congress.)

The three-hour funeral cortege up Pennsylvania Avenue to the Capitol was comprised of infantry, cavalry, marines, religious groups, and artillery. African American groups marched at the rear. With sabers glistening in the sun, the procession advanced amidst hoof beats, soulful dirges, and the lofty peal of bells from the towers of churches, firehouses, and schools. (Library of Congress.)

This is the hearse used to transport the casket to the Capitol, where Lincoln would lie in state for public viewing. The hearse was drawn by six horses. As it passed, mourners lining the procession route tossed spring blossoms—an impromptu occurrence at nearly all the funeral corteges across the country. (Author's collection.)

The myth persists that Abraham Lincoln did not want the railcar *United States* built, but in a *New York Times* interview given February 12, 1910, primary builder James T. Barkley said, "Lincoln would visit us two or three times a month during construction," adding, "Sitting on a sawhorse, he would suggest changes. There were many suggestions." (Library of Congress.)

Myron H. Lamson, superintendent of the Orange & Alexandria Railroad and intimately involved in construction of this car, dispelled the myth that Lincoln never rode in it alive. "This car was finished and run out over the Orange and Alexandria Railroad on a trial trip to Warrenton and pronounced a perfect success. On the trial trip were President Lincoln, Secretary of State Seward [and] General McCallum." (Library of Congress.)

After the funeral at the Capitol, the casket was brought to the Baltimore & Ohio Railroad station on Jersey Avenue, at left in this postwar photograph. The newly built locomotive No. 238—the *Edwin H. Jones*—steamed out with its nine-car consist at 8:00 a.m. on April 21, 1865. It followed 10 minutes behind the pilot train. (Library of Congress.)

The *United States* is about to cross the Potomac River to the Baltimore & Ohio Railroad station in the capital. On the platform is Myron Hawley Lamson, who was heavily involved in United States Military Railroad operations in Virginia. He helped build the car, modified it to receive Lincoln's casket, and even built the pyramid-shaped bier it would rest on. (Author's collection.)

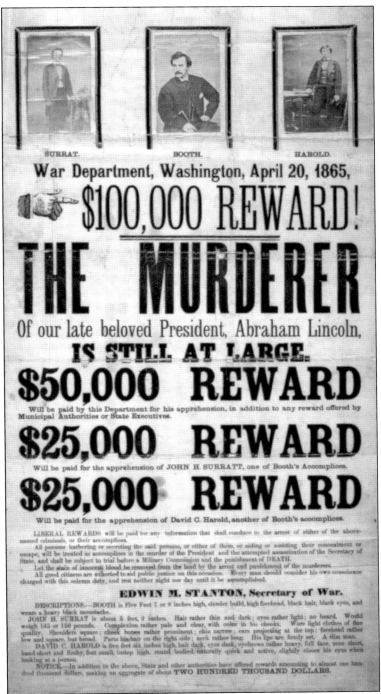

The wanted poster featuring huge rewards for the apprehension of John Wilkes Booth and his accomplices was printed with bold red, blue, and black inks and was the first to use actual photographs pasted to the poster. It contained warnings that anyone harboring these conspirators would be treated as accomplices. (Library of Congress.)

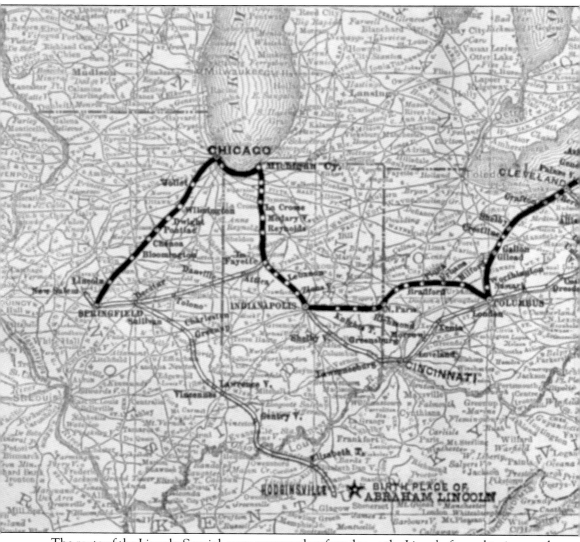

The route of the Lincoln Special, more commonly referred to as the Lincoln funeral train, was the reverse of Lincoln's inaugural train with some minor changes. Over 40 locomotives were involved in handling the funeral and pilot trains through seven states and 180 towns and cities, where its

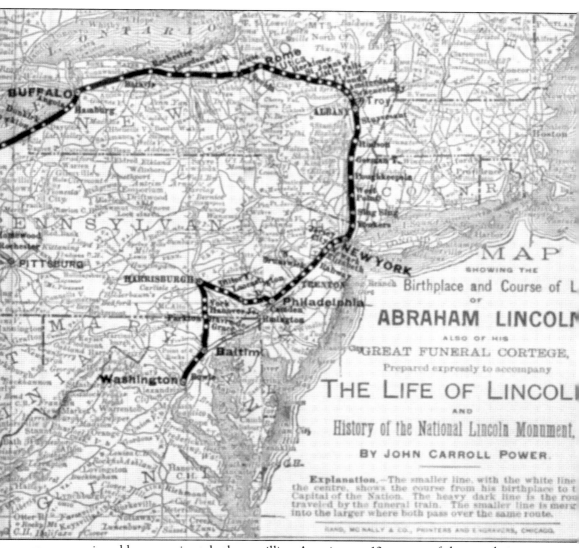

MAP

SHOWING THE

Birthplace and Course of L

OF

ABRAHAM LINCOLN

ALSO OF HIS

GREAT FUNERAL CORTEGE,

Prepared expressly to accompany

THE LIFE OF LINCOLN

AND

History of the National Lincoln Monument.

BY JOHN CARROLL POWER.

Explanation.—The smaller line, with the white line
the centre, shows the course from his birthplace to t
Capital of the Nation. The heavy dark line is the rou
traveled by the funeral train. The smaller line is merg
into the larger where both pass over the same route.

RAND, MC NALLY & CO., PRINTERS AND ENGRAVERS, CHICAGO.

passage was viewed by approximately three million Americans—10 percent of the population.
(Author's collection.)

The tried and condemned conspirators have nooses adjusted around their necks on the gallows in the yard of Washington's old Arsenal Penitentiary. From left to right are Mary Surratt (obscured), Lewis Powell, David Herold, and George Atzerodt. They were hanged at 1:26 p.m. on July 7, 1865. (Library of Congress.)

Federal agents tracked John Wilkes Booth to a tobacco barn on the Richard Garrett farm in Virginia where Boston Corbett, pictured here, shot and killed him. Corbett was an alcoholic who, after turning to God, grew his hair long to resemble Christ. After being propositioned by two prostitutes, he castrated himself. He will, however, be eternally remembered as the man who killed Lincoln's assassin. (Author's collection.)

Two

CHUGGING NORTH
BY NORTHWEST

The Baltimore
& Ohio Railroad
Camden Station
welcomed the train to
Baltimore, Maryland,
at 10:00 a.m. on
Friday, April 21.
Robert Lincoln was
aboard, having taken
the 38-mile trip from
Washington, but
immediately returned
to Washington
to be with his
distraught mother.
Camden Station had
welcomed Lincoln's
inaugural train,
and the president
also used it to get to
Gettysburg to give his
Gettysburg Address.
(Author's collection.)

Maryland was a slave state that stayed in the Union. Baltimoreans never wasted any love on Lincoln but were sensitive that his assassin was from their city. They kicked in thousands of dollars to the manhunt for John Wilkes Booth. The state was a major hub for the Union effort and was held under military occupation. The 6th Massachusetts Infantry is shown here bivouacked in Battle Monument Park in July 1861. (Library of Congress.)

Confederate prisoner Col. William S. Hawkins wrote of the assassination: "I desire . . . to Express my profound abhorrence of the deeds resulting in the death of President Lincoln. I wish also to mention that in passing through the prisons, where are still confined several thousand of my comrades, I heard from no one so fallen from the level of our common humanity as to be in any sense gratified at this atrocious murder." (Library of Congress.)

After removal of the casket from Camden Station, a procession delivered it to the Merchant's Exchange, pictured here, for public viewing. Baltimore, a major port city, commissioned J. Maximilian Godefroy and Benjamin Henry Latrobe to design the structure. Latrobe also designed the US Capitol in Washington. (Author's collection.)

Baltimore's Italianate-styled Philadelphia, Wilmington & Baltimore Railroad station was built of brick painted brown to look like stone. It did not shunt any of the Lincoln Special equipment but did bring participants to the city. It was here that a plot to kill Lincoln when his inaugural train arrived was foiled. His wife and children were spit at by an angry crowd as they were hurried away. (Wikimedia Commons.)

After viewing Lincoln's earthly remains at the Merchant's Exchange, the casket was taken to the Northern Central Railroad's Calvert Station, pictured here. The *United States* and an officers' car (also known as the "brass car") had been towed here from Camden Station, some say by mules, along the Baltimore Street Railroad. The train departed for Harrisburg, Pennsylvania, at 3:00 p.m. It would pass through many towns along the way. (Library of Congress.)

Part of a huge federal-run field hospital in York, Pennsylvania, this structure bears a simple garland of mourning. The hospital band played for the crowd as the funeral train arrived. Of the 14,000 sick and wounded treated here during the war, only 197 died. It was a remarkable survival rate for those days. (Author's collection.)

Daniel C. McCallum, whose portrait occupies the center of this lavishly decorated tender for the locomotive built in his honor, was superintendent of the United States Military Railroad and contributed to the planning and execution of the funeral and the train. This colorful artistry was typical of the Victorian age. (Author's collection.)

Situated along the train route through Pennsylvania was this quaint White Hall flag stop and telegraph station along the Pennsylvania Railroad main line. The tracks were moved in 1868. The structure survives. (Author's collection.)

A coal-burning locomotive and two cars are parked on the Northern Central Railroad tracks beside the station/hotel at Hanover Junction, Pennsylvania, in November 1863. The train was en route to Gettysburg with reporters and government officials to cover Lincoln's famous address. Lincoln's funeral train would roll through here on its way to Harrisburg. Increasingly, coaling stations were being added as locomotives transitioned to the new fuel. (Library of Congress.)

The impressive Pennsylvania Railroad station in Lancaster, Pennsylvania, seen in this postwar photograph, was beautifully decorated when the train arrived around 1:00 p.m. Newspapers reported 20,000 mourners had crammed the vicinity, but that was more than the city's population. Former president James Buchanan watched from his carriage. The train left slowly due to the press of mourners along the tracks. (Author's collection.)

Having crossed the Susquehanna River on the Cumberland Valley Railroad's bridge at Bridgeport, the train arrived in Pennsylvania's capital at Harrisburg around 8:30 p.m. on April 21. Few stations rivaled this one along the route. A pelting rain soaked the honor guard as well as those who followed the cortege down Market Street, then up State Street, and lastly into the capitol building. (Library of Congress.)

Porters brought along on the train would help new passengers board these sturdy and handsome Pennsylvania Railroad coaches. The list of passengers changed across each state border as some made connections back home and new dignitaries came aboard. (Library of Congress.)

The Pennsylvania Railroad's shiny new No. 331 has turned around at a nearby wye and is simmering at the head of the train, its water gauge at 125 pounds per square inch and ready for the engineer to ease the throttle into the 106-mile journey ahead. The pilot train, headed by No. 186, has already left with its single car carrying a road foreman, a trainmaster, and a few superintendents. (Library of Congress.)

This close-up of a boxcar that carried tools, spare parts for the *United States,* and luggage allows for an interesting sidebar to the saga of the train. Some accounts say that Willie Lincoln's casket was put in a boxcar prior to leaving Washington. The child's casket was placed in the front section of the *United States.* (Library of Congress.)

This detail from the photograph on the opposite page shows the modestly decorated Philadelphia & Reading Railroad station in the background, a mere stone's throw from the Pennsylvania Railroad station. (Library of Congress.)

Although the Philadelphia & Reading Railroad station at Harrisburg, pictured here in an 1862 stereo view, receives virtually no mention in the chronicles of the funeral train, the railroad certainly participated. Its timetables were altered, and it brought mourners to the funeral from the cities and towns it served. Also of singular importance is that the railroad was put under military control. (Library of Congress.)

This is the capitol building in Harrisburg where the president's remains were taken. The crowd filing past the coffin became so enormous people started opening windows and climbing out instead of waiting to exit through the tightly packed rear doors. (Library of Congress.)

The casket was removed from the hearse outside the capitol building and carried by the pallbearers to this catafalque in the Pennsylvania House of Representatives chamber. It was trimmed with white blossoms. The doors were opened at 9:00 p.m. for public viewing. At midnight, the undertaker, Dr. Charles D. Brown, closed the top part of the casket. (Author's collection.)

In a time when America was powered by wood, water, and whale oil (petroleum was still 20 years off), every scrap of wood was valuable. Behind this man stands a wood rick at the end of a station. It stored cordwood to fill locomotive tenders. Where ricks were not available, railroads placed piles of cordwood along the funeral route like primal offerings. (Library of Congress.)

The backhead controls inside elite passenger locomotive cabs, such as this period English version, were a tangle of copper and brass pipes, brass gauges with black lettering on white enameled faces, red turnoff knobs, and sometimes a few silvered trim pieces. Being a locomotive engineer was a prestigious profession. (Author's collection.)

A portrait of Lincoln was wired to the pilot cross bar on most of the locomotives used. American and state flags often flanked the portrait. Locomotive headlamps in those days had a flat glass lens. Illumination from an oil lamp reflected off a parabolic mirror providing some, but not much, light up the tracks. Ground glass lenses, like those used in lighthouses, were coming. (Author's collection.)

A view of the entire train is provided in this photograph taken on April 22 when it arrived at West Philadelphia. A small brass howitzer fired salutes while thousands filled the area to glimpse the train during its brief stay. Lincoln's portrait has been removed from No. 331. (Library of Congress.)

This detail of the West Philadelphia yard from the photograph above shows the officers' car and *United States* parked, as always, in tandem at the end of the train. A yard crew observes from the side. Small religious services close to the car were sometimes allowed during stops. Citizens were let inside. Groups of women often placed a flowered herald or wreath on the coffin. (Library of Congress.)

General Grant, an intended target of the conspirators, is shown wearing a mourning ribbon. He and his wife were the original guests of the Lincolns at Ford's Theater the night of April 14, but Julia Grant had them withdraw after becoming a victim of Mary Lincoln's acid tongue. The general tactfully informed the Lincolns they wanted to travel to New Jersey to see their children instead. (Author's collection.)

The Grants' Philadelphia home was spectacularly decorated for the funeral. General Grant must have had access to a storehouse of flags and military bunting. Stores across the country were quickly emptied of flags, black and white fabric, crepe, paint, tassels, fringe, poster board, and even black and white paper. Price gouging was rampant. (Author's collection.)

The Pennsylvania Railroad's No. 331 is parked in the West Philadelphia yard with the *United States* and officers' cars attached. The black bunting and flags needed freshening up, and the locomotive had its valves and drive rods oiled. It was common for a steam locomotive to average two hours of maintenance for every one hour of running time. (Author's collection.)

Obvious retouching was done to this photograph taken during Philadelphia's two-day hosting of the funeral train. They were fortunate they were sunny days. The train journey was a nightmare for photographers owing to its mostly nocturnal travel and the unrelenting rainstorms that followed it seemingly to add to its gloom. (Author's collection.)

All businesses were closed while Lincoln was to lie in state at Independence Hall. Bedlam broke out when angry citizens were forced to wait in line for over three hours while preferred citizens with passes were allowed into the hall ahead of them. Police are seen here holding the crowd back. A reporter wrote that it appeared the entire population of the city filled downtown. (Library of Congress.)

As the train moved up from West Philadelphia to its formal city arrival, the streets around the Philadelphia, Wilmington & Baltimore Railroad station, pictured here in 1865, were jammed with mourners. Hearts began pounding when two field gun blasts announced the arrival of the train as it glided into the station like a panting, glistening empress. (Courtesy of the Free Library of Philadelphia, Print and Picture Collection.)

Eleven divisions of soldiers and several bands accompanied the procession. Blasts from minute guns (a small field gun fired every minute as a salute) and the incessant pealing of bells echoed off the downtown buildings, adding drama to the event. At times, the streets were so clogged the procession had to be halted. (Library of Congress.)

This is a view toward Independence Hall where the president would lie in state for two days in the room where the US Constitution was debated and the Declaration of Independence signed. (Author's collection.)

In this stereo view, the honor guard seems imperiled as the press of mourners against the hearse intensifies during the procession down Broad Street. Regrettably, pickpockets were hard at work, as were thieves breaking into houses and stores while everyone was on or near Broad Street. (Library of Congress.)

This detail from the previous image shows the casket just as it is about to be removed by pallbearers and taken into Independence Hall. By midnight of the second day of viewing, an estimated 85,000 mourners had seen the remains. The line approached the casket and was then divided so two lines streamed by, one on either side, to speed things up. (Library of Congress.)

The cortege with its splendid horse-drawn hearse is parked on the cobblestone street near the hall. (Author's collection.)

These astonishing floral arrangements were placed around the catafalque. Flowers were an enormous part of the national funeral, from simple arrangements in home windows to pine boughs and fretted garlands draped inside stations where clocks were locked at 7:22—the moment Lincoln died. Flowered harps and crosses on stands were set beside the train route. Blossoms were pressed into diaries and saved as heirlooms. (Author's collection.)

Adm. David Glasgow Farragut was along as a pallbearer. He was famous for his battle cry of "Damn the torpedoes, full speed ahead!" during the August 1864 Battle of Mobile Bay. (Library of Congress.)

Three

DARKLY WEST

Reports of crowd sizes at the funeral stops often surpassed actual local populations. Nevertheless, the desire to be a part of this incredible event made people travel hundreds of miles. This ferry experienced large increases in ticket sales from people rushing to New York City to experience the mammoth procession and city hall viewing. (Library of Congress.)

The train traveled into New Jersey, making scheduled stops before arriving at the enormous Jersey City Ferry terminal along the Hudson River. A huge German musical association sang heartrending anthems and requiems in the waiting area, pictured here, bringing many listeners to tears. The *United States* was uncoupled and ferried across the Hudson River while the rest of the train maneuvered farther north. (Author's collection.)

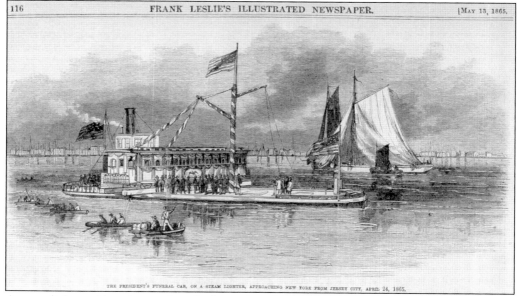

THE PRESIDENT'S FUNERAL CAR, ON A STEAM LIGHTER, APPROACHING NEW YORK FROM JERSEY CITY, APRIL 24, 1865.

A steam lighter with an impressive pilot house brought the *United States* across the Hudson, passing many ferry boats and ships with flags at half-staff. Some masts were bound with mourning cloth. Gun salutes were made by crews standing at attention. Steam whistles shrieked, and ship signal bells were noisily clanged in shows of respect. (Author's collection.)

The *United States* arrived at Manhattan's Debrosses Street Ferry. This detailed illustration shows crowds awaiting the procession to New York's city hall and the many ferries that brought mourners from afar. There is a hotel omnibus, a stagecoach, and even a small railroad ticket office that handled connections in the tri-state area. (Author's collection.)

A rare postwar photograph of a steam lighter, of sorts, is provided here, with a stern paddle wheel powered by a horizontal boiler and a large winch for lifting heavy cargoes off ships. There are no frills here like on the dolled-up Hudson River beauties. Right of center beyond this vessel is the Civil War monitor *Comanche*. (NH 71244, Naval History and Heritage Command.)

The honor guard flanks the hearse during the New York City procession. The uniforms apparently varied from robin's-egg blue to light gray depending on the states providing the guards. Many of these men were wounded or older soldiers unable to serve in battle. Lincoln's eight-handled studded coffin is visible in one of the clearest photographs of the funeral. (Library of Congress.)

A curious historical coincidence occurred during the procession as the hearse passed the Cornelius van Schaak Roosevelt mansion on New York City's Broadway. In the second story window are two young boys, one of which is young Teddy Roosevelt, a future president. This image is unique in that it contains a former and future president. (Library of Congress.)

Onlookers watch from the street and rooftops during New York City's massive procession. Prime viewing spots were sold for up to $100. After some controversy, African Americans were allowed to march. It is mentioned repeatedly that the funeral with its massive crowds was the first event where large groups of whites and African Americans were seen together. (Library of Congress.)

The Elmira Cornet Band of the 33rd New York State Volunteers provided dirges, hymns, and requiems for the procession. Many military units had their own bands to drill by, lead long marches, or hold up the rear. Often, at dusk, a single bugler or perhaps the entire band would play the lullaby "Taps" (written in 1862) as the camp's call to sleep. (Library of Congress.)

New Yorkers and
those with means to
take special trains
in from surrounding
states ascend the
steps of New York
City Hall to view
the president's
remains on display
in the rotunda. An
estimated 125,000
people passed
the open casket.
(Author's collection.)

Both darkly garlanded and festooned with colorful flags and silvered appointments, the New York City hearse was imperial in grandeur. Plumes of ostrich feathers, fringing of wound silvered wire, and black pennants cost the city $9,000. Building of the hearse was supervised by New York undertaker Peter Relyea, standing on the right with his stovepipe hat. (Library of Congress.)

Secretary Stanton strictly forbade any photographs of the corpse. He had those he learned of destroyed—all but this one, which he kept for himself. Photographing corpses was common in those days. There was an industry of producing photographs of dead children for grieving parents as a singular remembrance. (Author's collection.)

This detail from the previous image shows that only the upper part of the casket lid was opened during public showings. A flag was draped over the bottom part and covered with wreaths and flowers. (Author's collection.)

This illustration in *Frank Leslie's Illustrated Newspaper* depicts the arrival of President-elect Lincoln at New York City's Thirtieth Street Station on February 19, 1861. Such illustrations were created by talented craftsmen who meticulously carved layers of an image in blocks of Turkish boxwood. They were then converted by engravers into electrotyped copper plates for printing. (Library of Congress.)

This illustration depicts Lincoln's funeral train leaving the Hudson River Railroad's Thirtieth Street Station pulled by the *Union* locomotive. Lincoln had been the station's first official passenger when it opened specifically for the arrival of his inaugural train in 1861. (Author's collection.)

The *Union* American type 4-4-0 locomotive assumed responsibility of passage out of New York City and north up the Hudson Valley. (Author's collection.)

The historic Thirtieth Street Station is seen here in its waning days. (New York Central System Historical Society.)

Among the more ambitious funeral arches built over tracks to salute the train was this one at Ossining, New York. The *Union* drew the train under it as it passed Sing Sing Prison. Sing Sing is derived from the Native American *snick snick* meaning "stone upon stone." (Author's collection.)

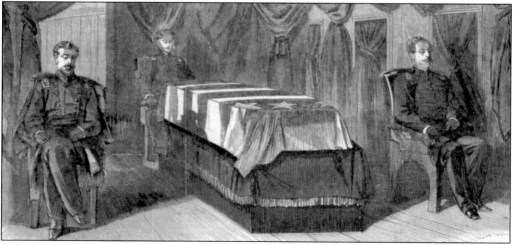

Myron Lamson oversaw the modification of the *United States* to accommodate the president's casket. He even built the pyramid-shaped bier to fasten it to. The iron railings on one of the end platforms was removed to allow easier handling. All coaches were illuminated during its night passage, making a lasting impression. (Author's collection.)

Places like Cold Spring, New York, afforded passengers glimpses of quaint towns and magnificent vistas of the Hudson River Valley, all viewed over the pitiful faces of mourners lining the tracks. Cold Spring, with its gabled station, was important to the war effort, having a foundry that produced astonishing quantities of munitions for the Union army as well as being a short boat ride from the US Military Academy at West Point. (Library of Congress.)

Salem, New York, lies farther into North Country near the Adirondacks—far from the train route. This 1865 carte de visite shows it decorated. Many towns were decorated after the Confederate surrender. It is not known if that is the case here or if it was for the assassination. One thing is for sure—1865 was a pivotal year for America. (Author's collection.)

West Point cadets pose on the lawn of the military academy. The academy produced 445 Civil War generals: 294 for the Union and 151 for the Confederacy. Among them were Robert E. Lee, James "Stonewall" Jackson, William Tecumseh Sherman, Ulysses S. Grant, and Jefferson Davis. A West Point graduate commanded one or both armies in every one of the 60 major battles; 105 were killed. (Library of Congress.)

In Garrison, New York, an important hotel and the ferry that provided service across the Hudson River to West Point are pictured in this Civil War–era stereo view. (Library of Congress.)

The shadow of the funeral train fell across this board-and-batten station, pictured in a postwar photograph in the hamlet of Garrison. It bears the dormer common on many of the stations along the New York Central Railroad's Hudson Valley main line. Garrison was important because it was across from West Point. This station has since been moved back from its original location. (Library of Congress.)

Essential to the war effort and the efficiency of the Lincoln national funeral was the US Military Telegraph Corporation. Established in 1861, several top telegraph engineers from the Pennsylvania Railroad were sent to Washington to serve in the newly created office. There was a telegraph operator with a portable telegraph machine in the officers' car of the funeral train. (Library of Congress.)

FOOT OF MAIDEN LANE. THE RAILROAD FERRY.

This illustration shows the ferry from East Albany that brought the casket across the Hudson River to Albany proper's railroad station. This waterway was a basin of sorts, which has since been filled in. (Author's collection.)

A crowd holding torches welcomed the train into East Albany at 11:00 p.m. on April 25. The coffin had already been ferried across the Hudson River to Albany. This photograph of the procession to city hall is blurred because of the long exposure needed. Night travel and gloomy rain unfortunately resulted in a limited photographic legacy of the funeral train. (Author's collection.)

The hearse with six white horses—each pair attended by a groom—waits beside Albany City Hall at Eagle and Washington Streets. Public viewing of the president went on for 12 hours starting at 1:15 a.m. Mourners passed the casket at the rate of 4,000 per hour, and thousands more standing in line outside were left disappointed when the doors were closed at 1:30 p.m. (Author's collection.)

Another view of the Albany procession to Albany City Hall for public viewing of the remains is provided here. New York secretary of state Chauncey M. Depew described the president lying in state: "The face had an expression of absolute content, of relief, at throwing off a burden such as few men have been called upon to bear—a burden which few could have borne." (Author's collection.)

Approximately 2,000 gathered at the depot in Schenectady, New York, shown in this postwar photograph, to glimpse the funeral train during its brief stop on April 26. It would then track west into the Mohawk Valley region. The structure in the foreground is the water tower used to fill tenders. This one is artfully done. Most were propped-up giant barrels or pump houses at creeks. (Author's collection.)

The train reached the Utica, New York, station, pictured in this postwar photograph, at 8:25 p.m. By then, many of the nation's telegraph lines were buzzing with news that Lincoln's assassin, John Wilkes Booth, had been killed at a Virginia tobacco farm. (Author's collection.)

This view of the Rome, Watertown & Ogdensburg Railroad station was taken after the war, but it was unchanged from when the funeral train came by on April 26. From Albany to Buffalo, it was a clear run on the New York Central Railroad because the amalgamation of 10 small railroads that comprised it had been standardized with four-foot, eight-and-one-half-inch track. (Author's collection.)

A stop was made at Auburn's New York Central Station, seen at left. Auburn prison looms in the background. The vintage 1840s pioneer-style locomotive was once a proud main line engine in Rochester but was now demoted to switching operations at the Auburn train yard. (Author's collection.)

The *J.L. Grant* headed the pilot train partially across upstate New York. This rare photograph of the handsome Taunton Locomotive Works locomotive, built in 1852, was taken at Cape Vincent, New York. Its unusual internal piston drive and early features were proudly maintained by the Rome, Watertown & Ogdensburg Railroad. The headlamp reads, "We Mourn Our Loss." (New York Central System Historical Society.)

The train rolled into Troy, New York, stopping at its massive Union Station, pictured here, on April 26. The tracks continued to be hemmed in by crowds through the cold nights. Faces of mourners were made more pitiful under bonfires and torchlight where they stood or knelt as the train passed. Sometimes locomotives were brought up to add illumination with their headlamps. (Author's collection.)

The 1839 through station at Syracuse, New York, in Vanderbilt Square received the train for a 15-minute stop at 11:15 p.m. A bell atop the station announced the train as it did every train's arrival. A crowd of heartbroken citizens braved the cold long enough to say goodbye to their beloved fallen president and then sent him on his way. (Author's collection.)

Syracuse held a procession and mock funeral complete with hearse and casket to coincide with Lincoln's funeral in Washington on April 19. The service was held in Hanover Square. Syracuse had deeper feelings because Secretary of State William H. Seward, attacked at the same time as Lincoln, was from the area and had earlier served as governor of New York. (Author's collection.)

71

Leaving West Syracuse, the train passed the New York Central Railroad shops, shown here in a postwar photograph. Yard crews are rarely mentioned, but they skillfully directed the train through the maze of tracks and switches as the consist was reconfigured. Using flags during the day and lanterns at night, they coordinated with the locomotive conductor making sure all was safe. (Author's collection.)

As the train steamed toward Rochester, New York, the distinguished *Dean Richmond*, pictured here at Rochester's Brown Street shops, was being readied for the run to Buffalo. Its firebox crackled as the engine idled. Engine crews reached long-necked oil cans into the drive rod linkage for one last squirt and screwed caps onto oil boxes after filling them. The locomotive was named for the president of the New York Central Railroad. (Author's collection.)

Arriving in Rochester at 3:20 a.m., the fallen president was in the absolute heart of abolitionism. Home to Frederick Douglas and Susan B. Anthony, the city welcomed Elizabeth Cady Stanton, Sojourner Truth, and Harriet Tubman to antislavery meetings. A band played, bells tolled, and the Genesee River falls bellowed beneath the train trestle as a loyal crowd thanked Lincoln for his sacrifice. (Author's collection.)

An important, though blurry, photograph of the lavishly decorated station at Batavia, New York, is one of few that shows mourners gathered at a station. The photographic process used then, known as wet-plate collodion, required spreading a cotton-based solution on a glass pane that, when exposed, created a negative. Conditions had to be nearly perfect for it to work. (Author's collection.)

The train arrived at Buffalo, New York, on Thursday, April 27, at 7:00 a.m. All passengers, including former president Millard Fillmore, who boarded at Batavia, got off, stretched their legs, and thought about breakfast since the train would be here all day. The round-roofed headhouse in the foreground was the original 1848 Exchange Street Station. The other sections seen in this postwar photograph were added later. (Author's collection.)

A hearse drawn by six white horses wearing black blankets wobbles through the throngs packing downtown Buffalo. It was said the mourners followed the remains like the ancient Egyptians would follow a beloved pharaoh to his tomb. The casket was displayed at St. James Hall, where 100,000 people, including former president Millard Fillmore and future president Glover Cleveland, passed by. (Author's collection.)

This photograph of H.D. Farwell's Coffin Ware Rooms at 13–15 Niagara Street provides a full view of the hearse with African American grooms attending the six white horses. Lincoln's spectacular funeral would prove a boon for the funeral industry nationwide, advancing technologies of embalming and preservation. (Collection of the Buffalo History Museum, general photograph collection, Presidents—Lincoln.)

The *Chauncey Vibbard*, pictured here at Rochester, had headed the inaugural train from Utica to Albany and was put in service for the funeral and pilot trains, sharing the same honor as the *Dean Richmond*, which also served on both journeys. American 4-4-0 locomotives were moving works of art with colorful frescoes, fleurs-de-lis, and brass appointments. They projected the prestige of the New York Central Railroad. (Author's collection.)

After leaving Buffalo, the Lincoln Special crossed briefly through northwestern Pennsylvania. Erie, Pennsylvania's Union Station, pictured here, was in the early stages of construction on the same footprint as its wooden predecessor. The Lincoln Special rolled into Erie at 2:50 a.m. and awaited the *William Chase* locomotive from the Cleveland, Painesville & Ashtabula Railroad to take it into Ohio. (Author's collection.)

The beautifully machined *David Upton* poses at the New York Central Railroad shops in Rochester. David Upton was superintendent of the railroad between Rochester and Buffalo and oversaw the funeral train's run between those two cities. It is assumed the man beside the tender is Upton. (Author's collection.)

Four

WEEPING BESIDE THE RUIN

"But if this country cannot be saved without giving up that principle, I was about to say I would rather be assassinated upon this spot than surrender it."

Columbia weeps beside the casket. The heroic goddess-like symbol derives her name from Christopher Columbus and represents the female personification of America. Reporters said tears fell heaviest when the casket was taken from the train to the hearse. One reporter called the casket "the ruin." A soldier and sailor also express their grief in this illustration. (Author's collection.)

Among the most iconic photographs of this amazing event is the highly decorated *Nashville* at Cleveland, Ohio's Union Station. This proud and colorful engine and tender has been polished and serviced for the next leg of the journey. (Library of Congress.)

Cleveland to Columbus. Saturday. April 29th, 1865.

Leave Cleveland	12.00	Midnight
Berea	12.13	A. M.
Olmstead	12.51	"
Columbia	1.02	"
Grafton	1.23	"
La Grange	1.37	"
Wellington	2.00	"
Rochester	2.17	"
New London	2.36	"
Greenwich	2.39	"
Shiloh	3.19	"
Shelby	3.39	"
Crestline	4.07	"
Galion	4.23	"
Iberia	4.41	"
Gilead	5.05	"
Cardington	5.20	"
Ashley	5.43	"
Eden	5.55	"
Berlin	6.19	"
Lewis Centre	6.32	"
Orange	6.17	"
Worthington	6.36	"
Arrive Columbus	7.30	A. M.

The Cleveland-to-Columbus timetable put out by the Cleveland, Columbus & Cincinnati Railroad shows the precise night schedule. Piles of wood were left trackside for immediate pickup by the funeral train. The train steamed into the night, passing through lantern-lit towns and countrysides illuminated in the orange glow of bonfires. With the arrival of the pilot train, hearts would pound and tears would fall, because the funeral train was only 10 minutes behind. (Library of Congress.)

The locomotive at left in this view of the Cleveland, Columbus & Cincinnati Railroad yard was involved in assembling the train for the next leg of the trip. All locomotives here are of the rarer internal drive type. (Author's collection.)

The *Chicago* of the Cleveland, Columbus & Cincinnati Railroad is credited with participating in switching operations while the train was maneuvered in Cleveland. (Author's collection.)

The Cleveland funeral committee, realizing there was no building large enough to accommodate the thousands expected to view the president, had this beautiful pagoda-style pavilion built in Monument Square. (Author's collection.)

A serene view of the funeral rites in Cleveland is captured in this photograph. (Author's collection.)

The man at far right in the light-colored coat is either the photographer or assistant in this photograph at Cleveland's Union Station. Photographers often wore long coats with lots of pockets. (Author's collection.)

This view outside the Iowa state house was taken on April 19 during the nationwide memorial service. (Author's collection.)

The funeral train, pulled by the *Nashville*, rolled out of Cleveland at midnight and traveled through the night, arriving on April 29 at 7:30 a.m. at Columbus Union Station, pictured here. Passengers appreciated the amenities of the National Hotel while the president lay in repose at the Columbus state house. Funeral committees made sure meals were prepared at extended stops. (Author's collection.)

A large flag is suspended from the bell tower of the Butler Street School in Bryan, Ohio, in a show of respect for the fallen president in this postwar postcard. (Author's collection.)

Entertainer Seth Kinman once entertained the Lincoln family with a fiddle made from a mule's skull. He marched in Lincoln's funeral processions as far as Columbus, shouldering his famous long rifle "Ol' Cottonblossum." He made chairs from animal pieces for several presidents. This one was for Andrew Johnson. (Library of Congress.)

Two officials at the United States Military Railroad headquarters in Alexandria display chains for their pocket watches. Railroads had jewelers to keep quality 17-jewel pocket watches in perfect working order. Before time standardization, time could differ up to 15 minutes between locations, leading to terrible train collisions. Coordination of the funeral train from the United States Military Railroad kept it safe and on time. Railroad activists ultimately standardized time zones nationwide. (Library of Congress.)

Heavy rains had ended when the train pulled into Columbus. This 17-foot-long hearse brought the casket down High Street to the state house for services. "LINCOLN" was emblazoned in silver letters on both sides of the vehicle. Mourners tossed spring flowers into High Street as the hearse passed. (Author's collection.)

The procession has stopped as the casket is taken from the hearse and carried up the walkway to the state house. Columbus was one of 11 cities to organize a major processional funeral. (Author's collection.)

Onlookers on the walkway in front of the Ohio capitol building watch the throng of mourners slowly entering to pay their respects. The massive Greek Doric columns of the colonnade are bound with black fabric. The pediment has a plaque that reads, "With malice to no one, with charity for all." (Author's collection.)

An impressive illustration of the Columbus obsequies captures the dignity and reverence of the event. (Author's collection.)

The flower-covered casket in the rotunda of the Columbus state house rested on a simple bier. Many who viewed the casket in its varied locations associated the fragrance of lilacs and violets with the funeral years later. The emotions evoked by this led some to be repulsed by the fragrances of spring blossoms—especially lilacs. (Author's collection.)

The First National Bank of Columbus in downtown Columbus was boldly decorated for the funeral. All businesses were ordered closed. The ones that stayed open to protest Lincoln's policies drew the wrath of outraged citizens, who broke windows and beat employees. (Author's collection.)

The *Louisville* of the Cleveland, Columbus & Cincinnati Railroad was assigned pilot train duties out of Cleveland. These engines were often buffed to high luster with "waste," a solution of cotton strands soaked in oil that was primarily wadded and packed into axle journal boxes on trucks for lubrication. Apparently, it also did a fine job as a cleaning agent. (Author's collection.)

The train arrived in Indianapolis, Indiana, at 7:00 a.m. on April 30 on the Columbus & Indiana Railroad 15 days after the assassination. Downtown Indianapolis was decorated with "habiliments of grief" and thronged with Hoosiers. The city band played the "Lincoln Funeral March" while plumed horses carried the hearse to the state house. (Author's collection.)

The *Indianapolis Daily Gazette* wrote about "the funeral procession, the solemn dirges, and, above all, the patient multitude that stood for hours in the drenching rain waiting an opportunity to look upon the earthly tenement so lately vacated by the spirit." This photograph, taken during the mock funeral, is representative of that event. (Author's collection.)

This closer look at the hearse with its honor guard was likely taken during the mock funeral held at the time of the national funeral. (Author's collection.)

An impromptu memorial occurred on May 1 when the train rolled to a stop beneath the wonderfully garlanded arch at Michigan City, Indiana. It was to be a brief affair with no long-winded eulogies—something that was originally telegraphed to all stops to keep the train on schedule. (Author's collection.)

This soaring arch at Michigan City was 30 feet tall and fretted with evergreen boughs, roses, and other floral wreaths. The sign read, "Though dead he yet speaketh." The loss of Lincoln's leadership to help heal the nation troubled many already worried about America's uncertain future. (Author's collection.)

Freed slaves leave Richmond, Virginia, on a canal barge with the burned city looming behind them. While the funeral train chugged halfway across America, the reality of the social displacement caused by the war and the assassination were being realized. Lincoln wanted full citizenship rights for freed slaves, and would never have allowed the abuses they were subjected to. He likely would have smashed the Ku Klux Klan. (Library of Congress.)

The nearly unbearable need to be a part of this event was carried to extremes even as far west as San Francisco. In this stereo view, a procession with a hearse makes its way through the city. In a time of deep religiosity, the individual and nation had to reconcile how a benevolent God would allow the war's carnage and then the assassination. (Library of Congress.)

A fashionable Boston library displays tastefully fringed valances of mourning fabric in this stereo view. The banner reads, "A Nation Mourns Him Who Has Honored It." New England governors begged for the train to be rerouted through their states, but to no avail. (Author's collection.)

A photograph taken on April 16, 1865, shows many African Americans in Vicksburg, Mississippi, reacting to news of Lincoln's murder. Larger Southern cities were under Union occupation and respect for the martyred president was demanded in newspaper reporting and eulogies. Even without warnings, some of the most touching eulogies came from the Southern ministers. African Americans stood to lose the most from the assassination. (Author's collection.)

Poet Walt Whitman greatly admired Lincoln and was deeply affected by his assassination. He wrote "Oh Captain! My Captain!" along with other poems and elegies about the fallen president. He gave lectures on the assassination and train and included a selection of his Lincoln writings in his critically acclaimed *Leaves of Grass*. (Library of Congress.)

A large crowd has gathered in Court House Square in Bloomington, Illinois, to participate in an "indignation meeting" to express grief and anger over the assassination. There were many of these meetings held around the country. (Author's collection.)

Detroit's Martius Square hosted a mock funeral on April 25 that included a procession and memorial service. Not everyone was sad about Lincoln's death. Millions of people both North and South hated him, but they kept silent during demonstrations such as this. Regardless of the distance from the train, there was much duress and genuine sadness in these events. (Author's collection.)

Posing in front of their Detroit firehouse, the crew of fire engine No. 3, bedecked with strands of crepe, were proudly represented in their mock funeral. (Author's collection.)

A Union soldier grieves for a friend who perished in a Richmond prison camp. These hastily dug graves with their simple markers certainly contrasted with the pageantry of President Lincoln's send-off going on up North. Sadly, and to the unending pain of families, many soldiers' bodies were left to rot on battlefields. (Library of Congress.)

This family stayed together during the war. The social upheavals of the conflict were profound. Thousands of widows and orphans were left destitute. In the South, children and elderly died from hunger and disease at terrifying rates. In civil wars, the battlefield and home blend in nightmarish realities. Uncounted civilian deaths and soldiers dying years later from wounds put the actual death rate near 800,000. (Library of Congress.)

While memorials were underway at Chicago's Cook County Courthouse, the empty train was moved via the Galena & Chicago Union Railroad to the Chicago & Alton Railroad station at Canal Street. The circuitous route of the train in and out of Chicago required precision maneuvering across four railroads—a manageable task in the city that was the rail center of America. (Library of Congress.)

UPON THE MOMENT OF THE ARRIVAL OF THIS SACRED RELIC IN THE CITY

FOURTEEN SALUTES FROM CANNON

WILL BOOM FORTH A WELCOME

One for each letter forming the name

ABRAHAM LINCOLN

and one following each hour throughout the entire day.

Bands will Play National and Sacred Airs, and Bells will Toll

The Public are requested to join in this demonstration in honor of the event and in memory of the

WORLD'S GREATEST CHARACTER

Hang Out Flags and Drape Your Homes in Mourning.

BE AN AMERICAN

and instill into your children and your children's children the principles of this great and good man.

"With Malice Toward None. With Charity For All"

CHICAGO AND ALTON R. R.   THE ONLY WAY.

The Chicago & Alton Railroad issued this stern broadside regarding the arrival of the train and the etiquette that was expected. (Author's collection.)

Accounts say the Chicago & Alton Railroad locomotive No. 58 clanged its bell as it backed the funeral train on to the Michigan Central Railroad trestle along Chicago's waterfront. This is one of the few photographs showing the entire train. A young engineer wrote that, during his operation of the Lincoln Special locomotive, he clanged the bell on the count of eight: "1, 2, 3, 4, 5, 6, 7, Clang! 1, 2, 3, 4, 5, 6, 7, Clang!" (Author's collection.)

Chicago & Alton Railroad locomotive No. 58, handsomely bedecked, cleaned, oiled, and fueled, is photographed presumably at the Canal Street depot. Entry of the Lincoln Special into Chicago involved the Michigan Central Railroad, the Chicago & Alton Railroad, the Illinois Central Railroad, and the Galena & Chicago Union Railroad. This locomotive would handle the last leg of the journey to Springfield. (Authors collection.)

This 1860s photograph captures Chicago's massive waterfront railroad facilities. The Illinois Central Railroad station is to the left. The Lincoln Special was backed out onto the Michigan Central Railroad trestle. (Author's collection.)

The fortress-like Great Central Station of the Illinois Central Railroad was the largest building in downtown Chicago upon its completion in 1856. The funeral train was driven alongside this headhouse on May 1 and backed out onto the Michigan Central Railroad trestle on the lake, where it remained during the memorial ceremonies. (Author's collection.)

The *United States* is parked on the Michigan Central Railroad trestle during the Chicago services under the watchful gaze of the ever-vigilant honor guard. Lake Michigan is in the background. The car had performed well except for a few issues of easing the four trucks through switch tracks. Some said the car was noisy and a bit of a rough rider because of all the wheels. (Library of Congress.)

Some castings for the trucks were made from burst Civil War shells. The harp-shaped guides featured patriotic flourishes that were painted red, white, and blue. The wide wheel treads intended to accommodate different track gauges occasionally made for a rough ride because the car slid from side to side. (Library of Congress.)

An opportunity for the Pullman company presented itself when its first luxurious sleeping car was added in Chicago for the last stretch to Springfield. Lincoln family members and friends rode it. These cars were nearly double the cost of standard passenger cars. The *Pioneer's* best days were behind it in this postwar photograph. Robert Lincoln would eventually become the Pullman company's president. (Author's collection.)

Chicago gave the slain president a grander send-off than New York City or Washington. The fashionable row houses at Chicago's Park Row are filled with onlookers as the procession assembles on Michigan Avenue. The soaring arch spanning Michigan Avenue and courthouse decorations alone cost $15,000. A temporary train depot was constructed to receive the casket from the funeral car. (Author's collection.)

Thirty-six young women in white, representing each of the states, followed the hearse. There were 34 states when the war started in 1861. West Virginia, which broke off from Virginia, was admitted in 1863, having the distinction of being the first state to secede from the Confederate States of America. Nevada was admitted in 1864. (Library of Congress.)

The hearse is making its way to the Cook County Courthouse, led by a huge procession. (Library of Congress.)

The procession arrived at the Cook County Courthouse on May 1. The streets around the building were thronging with mourners. Chicago had strong ties to Lincoln; as a lawyer, he visited the city over 20 times to handle legal and political issues. The *Chicago Tribune* had a strong Republican voice and greatly admired Lincoln. (Author's collection.)

A steady line of mourners anxious to see the remains makes its way up the courthouse steps through the open doors. Viewing started at 6:00 p.m. and continued through the night. As many as 7,000 mourners passed the casket in two lines each hour. (Library of Congress.)

The braver souls within the Chicago funeral committee used heroic efforts to decorate the colonnaded tower over the Cook County Courthouse. The smaller bell tower originally announced to the city that the Lincoln funeral train had arrived. (Library of Congress.)

This illustration depicts the scene inside the Cook County Courthouse. Exposure to air and dust and the jostling by a long train ride quickened the deterioration of Lincoln's corpse. The *Columbus Crisis* editor wrote, "A dark, unnatural face whose features were plaintive and pinched and sharp, piteously like death." The undertaker increasingly applied more makeup. (Author's collection.)

Five

RETURN TO THE WILDERNESS

The Lincolns' Springfield home was draped in mourning. Lincoln had come from the wilderness of the Midwest to rise from a rugged childhood to a larger-than-life figure admired worldwide. His return as a martyred president who freed a race from slavery brought him back from sophisticated eastern cities to the wilderness of his youth. (Author's collection.)

The train stopped at the Great Western Railroad depot in Springfield on May 3. This image shows the depot before the second story was added. It was here that Lincoln gave a heartfelt speech to the community before his inaugural train left for Washington. It was the last time he saw his town. (Author's collection.)

The law office where Lincoln launched his political career is seen here draped in funeral bunting. (Author's collection.)

The Springfield hearse was among the finest. It was brought in from St. Louis, being the only four-horse hearse in the Midwest. Adorned with plumes of ostrich feathers and gold, silver, and crystal ornamentation, it glittered. Hearses were among the most sophisticated vehicles built in those days. (Library of Congress.)

Mourners linger near Springfield's Chicago & Alton Railroad station on Jefferson Street. The pilot train rolled in at 8:50 a.m., with the funeral train chugging in 10 minutes later. (Author's collection.)

The Lincolns' back parlor is decorated in mourning bunting in this stereo view. (Author's collection.)

When the Lincolns left Springfield for Washington, they gave their dog Fido to a neighbor. Fido was brought out for the funeral. The president loved animals, especially kittens. Secretary Seward gave the Lincolns two kittens early in their first term. (Author's collection.)

Lincoln's Horse "Old Bob."

Variously called Old Bob or Old Robin, Lincoln's Springfield horse was used in the funeral cortege, led as a riderless horse. The family home, in full funeral regalia, is in the background. (Author's collection.)

On a happier day, Lincoln is shown on the front lawn of the family home with his sons. (Author's collection.)

With approximately 600,000 men killed in a gruesome civil war, Lincoln won reelection. Every successive generation has reinterpreted him. It was his singular inspiring declaration, however, that stands eternal, "that we here highly resolve that these dead shall not have died in vain, that this nation, under God, shall have a new birth of freedom, and that government of the people, by the people, for the people, shall not perish from the earth." (Library of Congress.)

Mary Lincoln never recovered from the loss of her husband. Declining mental health caused her son Robert to institutionalize her. Mary was a difficult mother-in-law, and Robert's wife would not speak to her. Newspapers made her a laughingstock. She died July 16, 1883, of a stroke at age 63. She remains one of America's most interesting and tragic figures. (Library of Congress.)

The loss of William Wallace "Willie" Lincoln to typhoid in 1862 was the biggest heartbreak for the Lincoln family. For students of the Lincolns, this amazing American family, with its triumphs and tragedies, refuses to dissolve into the ether of time. (Author's collection.)

The Globe Tavern, home to the Lincolns as newlyweds, is prominent in this view of downtown Springfield. Pallbearers and other dignitaries are gathered beside the tavern. (Library of Congress.)

There were a surprising number of Lincoln look-alikes among the pallbearers and attendants. (Library of Congress.)

This view is looking up Springfield's Adams Street. The arrow points to the Lincoln-Herndon law firm where Lincoln practiced law with partner Stephen T. Logan in a third-floor office. That partnership dissolved in 1844, and Lincoln took on William H. Herndon as a junior partner. (Author's collection.)

The First Presbyterian Church was where the Lincolns worshiped when they lived in Springfield. In towns and cities nationwide, eulogies for the fallen president ranged from magnificent to ridiculous, such as asserting God killed Lincoln because he was in a sinful theater. Some of the most heartfelt eulogies came from Southern churches. (Author's collection.)

The funeral committee of 150 members spent 10 days decorating Springfield's capitol building. They used up to 1,500 yards of black and white goods. (Author's collection.)

The Globe Tavern in downtown Springfield is where the Lincolns rented a room for $4 a week after their marriage in 1842. Their son Robert was born here. The tavern served as offices for several stagecoach lines. A clerk would ring a bell on the roof to alert stablemen that a stage was arriving, so they could tend the horses. (Author's collection.)

Victor Wheeler was 17 when he and his friend Isaac "Ike" Andrew were tasked with decorating the dome because of their agility and indifference to working at such heights. They did a remarkable job fastening the long streamers and rosettes. (Library of Congress.)

A view of downtown Springfield during the funeral is provided in this stereo view. (Author's collection.)

A large, patient crowd awaits entrance through the capitol's north door to view the remains. (Author's collection.)

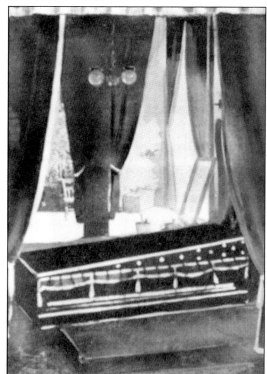

This bier, built on an angle to allow easier viewing of the remains, is made sadder by this being the Springfield capitol where Lincoln gave his famous "House Divided" speech in 1858. (Author's collection.)

Abraham Lincoln's casket and that of his son Willie were placed in this holding vault at Springfield's Oak Ridge Cemetery. The moment of their placement here effectively brought an end to the national funeral. All crepe was unraveled from the trains in preparation of sending them back to their railroads. Passengers made connections to return home. (Author's collection.)

Guards watch over the holding vault at Oak Ridge Cemetery. It was also known as the Mathers Vault. A more fitting tomb and memorial was in the design stage, and in 1871, the remains of Lincoln and his three youngest sons were placed in crypts in the yet unfinished tomb. (Library of Congress.)

The Lincoln Tomb, completed in 1874, has undergone numerous repairs and renovations. It holds the bodies of Abraham, Mary, Willie, Edward, and Thomas in a 10-foot-deep concrete vault. Robert Lincoln was buried in Arlington National Cemetery. (Library of Congress.)

Lincoln's remains were moved 17 times due to badly needed repairs to the tomb. The casket was eventually sealed in a steel-lined chamber and covered with cement to prevent attempts to steal the corpse. (Library of Congress.)

Mary Lincoln approved this gimmicky image of her husband's hands on her shoulders. Religious superstitions were powerful in a time when seances and spiritual mediums were commonly used to contact the dead. Mary was criticized over this. Nevertheless, it evoked a deep emotional response from many. (Author's collection.)

This photograph of a woman crying in a chair similar to the one Lincoln was shot in captures the pathos of the day. A cottage industry of Lincoln memorial products quickly sprang up, and the president's lavish funeral revolutionized the funeral business in America. (Author's collection.)

Among the souvenirs that quickly sprang up was this carte de visite titled "The Apotheosis of Lincoln." In it, the president is welcomed to heaven by George Washington, who holds a laurel wreath over his head. In theology, apotheosis is the elevation from human to divine status. Lincoln was elevated, in the minds of many, to an American saint. (Author's collection.)

President Johnson and General Grant are seated in the front row of this grandstand to observe the grand review of the Union army held May 23–24, 1865. Johnson declared a formal end to the war on May 10. He felt a celebration using the available elements of the Union army would pick up people's spirits. (Library of Congress.)

Mourning ribbons were a popular way to connect with others in the collective grief of the nation. This boy, in military dress, wears a mourning ribbon. This show of grief continued for weeks after the funeral. (Author's collection.)

Crowds line both sides of Pennsylvania Avenue in Washington, DC, to watch the grand review wherein the Union army was honored. (Library of Congress.)

In another view of the grand review, there are far fewer people wearing black mourning dress. The mirth that had left the land half a decade ago in the lead-up to the war seemed to be slowly returning. While a lot lay ahead for the wounded nation, things were getting back to normal. (Library of Congress.)

In 1866, the Union Pacific Railroad ran an excursion to the point where the 100th meridian crossed its main line in Nebraska. It included the recently acquired *United States* car. Pawnee warriors pose with the excursionists, including future president Rutherford B. Hayes. (Author's collection.)

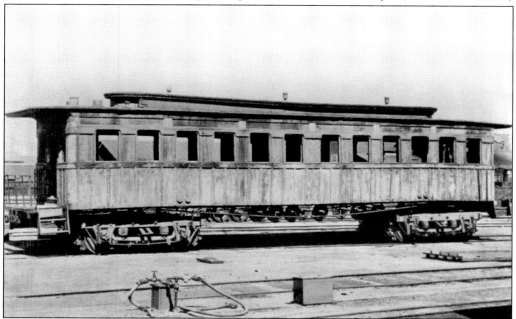

The *United States* passed through several owners who promised to restore it but instead subjected it to reckless stewardship. Here, it has been converted into a camp car. The paint is worn down to bare wood. The four sets of trucks have been replaced with two sets. The inside was gutted of its unique cabinetry. It was once considered America's most sacred relic, but thoughtless owners felt otherwise. (Author's collection.)

Onlookers and souvenir seekers rummage through the charred remains of the *United States*. It had been stored in a flimsy shed just north of Minneapolis at Columbia Heights on Thirty-seventh Avenue. The car burned during an extensive grass fire on March 18, 1911. (Photograph by Carl Lewis; courtesy Richard Lewis.)

Lincoln's private car lived on in history and legend, however, as evidenced in this postcard for the 42nd national encampment of the Grand Army of the Republic. (Author's collection.)

This arch was built for a victory parade held nearly three months after Lincoln's death. Spanning Rochester, New York's, Four Corners, it represented the emotional end of the war, although there was still much to deal with. Nonetheless, it was time to move forward and turn thoughts to peaceful reunification. (Author's collection.)

Robert Lincoln (1843–1926) is pictured on May 30, 1922, at the dedication of the Lincoln Memorial in Washington, DC. Although he was not at his father's assassination, he was, by strange historical coincidences, present at the shootings of Presidents James Garfield and William McKinley. He became president of the Pullman Palace Car Company. (Library of Congress.)

Former acting president of the Confederacy Jefferson Davis outlived Lincoln, his Yankee rival, by nearly a quarter of a century. He is pictured here shortly before his death in 1889. (Author's collection.)

Jessie Harlan (Lincoln) Beckwith (1875–1948) was the last surviving descendant to carry Lincoln's surname. When her son Robert Todd Lincoln Beckwith died in 1985, the family line became extinct. (Wikimedia Commons.)

In 1862, Lincoln authorized construction of the Transcontinental Railroad not just for industry but for other purposes that included quieting talk the West might pull away from the fractious nation embroiled in civil war. Completion of the railroad in 1869 did much to unite the nation. (Library of Congress.)

Hundreds of battlegrounds, museums, reenactments, statues, and books keep the Civil War era reachable. Sometimes the efforts are extraordinary, such as in New Freedom, Pennsylvania's, Steam into History, a Civil War heritage museum that offers rides on a replica Civil War train. It is pictured here at Hanover Junction along the original Northern Central Railroad main line where the Lincoln funeral train traveled. A replica of the *United States* car exists elsewhere. (Author's collection.)

BIBLIOGRAPHY

Collea, Joseph D. Jr. *New York and the Lincoln Specials: The President's Pre-Inaugural and Funeral Trains Cross the Empire State*. Jefferson, NC: McFarland & Company, 2018.

Donald, David Herbert. *Lincoln*. New York, NY: Simon and Schuster, 1996.

Faust, Drew Gilpin. *This Republic of Suffering: Death and the American Civil War*. New York, NY: Vintage Books, 2008.

Leavy, Michael. *The Lincoln Funeral: An Illustrated History*. Yardley, PA: Westholme Publishing, 2015.

———. *The New York Central System*. Charleston, SC: Arcadia Publishing, 2008.

Mingus, Scott L. Sr. *"A Carnival of Grief": The Lincoln Funeral Train in Pennsylvania*. Self-published, 2022.

Stevens, Barlow Walter. *A Reporter's Lincoln*. Lincoln, NE: University of Nebraska Press, 1998.

Swanson, James L. *Bloody Crimes: The Funeral of Abraham Lincoln and the Chase for Jefferson Davis*. New York, NY: Harper Perennial, 2010.

White, John H. *A History of the American Locomotive: Its Development, 1830–1880*. New York, NY: Dover Publications, 1979.

DISCOVER THOUSANDS OF LOCAL HISTORY BOOKS FEATURING MILLIONS OF VINTAGE IMAGES

Arcadia Publishing, the leading local history publisher in the United States, is committed to making history accessible and meaningful through publishing books that celebrate and preserve the heritage of America's people and places.

Find more books like this at
www.arcadiapublishing.com

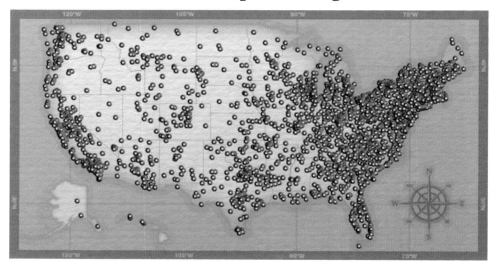

Search for your hometown history, your old stomping grounds, and even your favorite sports team.

Consistent with our mission to preserve history on a local level, this book was printed in South Carolina on American-made paper and manufactured entirely in the United States. Products carrying the accredited Forest Stewardship Council (FSC) label are printed on 100 percent FSC-certified paper.

MADE IN THE